Song of Lilith

SONG

OF

Lilith

Andrew Chiniche

Reflective
Light
Press

Song of Lilith by Andrew Chiniche

Published by Reflective Light Press
Copyright © 2023 Andrew Chiniche

First Edition: April 2023
Printed in the United States of America

Paperback ISBN: 979-8-9880227-0-1
Hardback ISBN: 979-8-9880227-1-8

Edited by Eva Zen
Cover by Frina Art

Song of Lilith

I.
In the Beginning

I. And God Created Woman

As the Word speaks into space,
the breath of God vibrates,
awaking my flesh from clay,
and it is good.

The air as it moves over my lips
inflates my lungs
causing my chest to rise.

My heart beats,
pumping blood through my veins,
bringing a flush to my cheeks.

A chill on the breeze
caresses my naked skin.
My hair follicles stir.

I open my eyes,
and the brightness of light
floods into my retinas.

The azure sky stretches
above me in all directions.
I feel small in an infinite expanse of space.

Through my nose, I breathe
in the aroma of cherry blossoms
mixed with rich soil.

I reach my arms towards the sun
and embrace its warmth.

In a bower, on the edge of a meadow,
the tall grasses tickle as they sway.
Everything is fresh and new.

The song of the earth,
through the parakeet's twitter
and the wind's whisper,
fills my mind with knowledge.

"You are Lilith,
first of your kind.

Along with your partner, Adam,
you are created to care for this paradise
and to populate the world.

You are the All-Mother."

I stand and saunter towards a bubbling brook
finding Adam asleep on the ground.
The herbage cradles him like a nest.

Chestnut hair frames his face
and his skin glows bronze,
reflecting traces of the sun.

His muscles ripple
with a secret strength,
calling out for my touch.

His flaccid manhood
lies hidden in his bush,
its head peeking out.

While my eyes pore over him,
I picture what I look like;
We must be a reflection of one another.

As I mindlessly stroke my hair
that flows like fire through my fingers,
I imagine our future together.

As husband and wife,
we roam paradise:
tending the land,
caring for our children,
and sharing our knowledge.

His stirring breaks my reverie,
and I retreat behind a white oak,
my stomach a bundle of nerves.

After a few moments,
I find my internal courage
and reveal myself.

"Hello, Adam."
A mumbled acknowledgment floats to my ears.

I feel his gaze harvest the curves of my body:
exploring my hips, lingering on my breasts.

In a fumbling embrace,

the heat of his skin speaks to mine.

Natural instinct takes over:
I am lowered to the earth,
and he finds his way into my sacred slot.
I am hung on his rood.

With a series of quick thrusts,
I am deflowered.

He rolls off me onto his side
and drifts to sleep.

As his seed drips down my inner thigh,
a newly discovered fire burns
unquenched through my body.

Probing with my fingers,
I discover a delicate velvet orchid
budding between my legs.

Moving with a deliberate motion,
I coax the petals open,
my nerves a live circuit.

Biting my inner cheeks to stifle my pleasure,
I unleash a deluge of pent-up emotion
and see the face of God.
My fingers glisten with expended dew.

With a satisfied smile,
I wrap myself around Adam
and join him in his slumber.

II. End of the Honeymoon

The full moon crests for a third time,
and our life together has grown rigid,
our story not moving forward.

Although he does enjoy his use of me,
he is overbearing
and not open to our partnership.

The time has come to exert myself.
We were created as equals,
not as a servant and her master.

The first rays of the rising sun
peek over the horizon,
awaking me to the dawn.

Adam lies on his back in deep slumber,
oblivious that morning has arrived.

My name arises on a soft moan,
and his body trembles.
He must be dreaming.

I crawl over to check on him.
A fleshy tower stands,
casting dawn's shadow over his stomach.

A wet warmth spreads from my loins,
radiating over my body
and swelling in my breasts.
I will have *my* pleasure.

Taking him into my mouth,
I coax my lips over his veiny shaft
and hug it with my tongue.

With each bob of my head,
I feel his hardness increase.

Pushing to his root,
I breathe in his musk,
his mass slightly choking me.

I need him inside me.

So, I position myself in a squat
and guide his cock with a loose grip.

Teasing with his bulbousness,
I run his head over my opening,
my lips parting in welcome.

With a soft push,
his rod enters me,
traveling into my creamy corridor.

I sit flat and relish his throbbing mass

as it mingles with my pulse.
I squeeze with a tight grip.
He stirs as his dream becomes reality.

With my hands on his chest for leverage,
I grind into his pelvis
and pump my hips on his hardness.

As my breath quickens,
meaty slaps echo around the bower.

Living on the edge of ecstasy,
a shiver courses through my being.
An awakened Adam becomes my toy.

As he thrusts in time with my movement,
I feel his hands fumble over my breasts,
fondling my stiff nipples with his thumbs.

I close my eyes
and picture my core:
a line of power expands
from my brain to my groin.

A spontaneous rush explodes,
my sex tightens and, in a liquid gush,
my indulgence releases a generous moan.

I collapse over Adam,
and he slips out of me,
not yet achieving his satisfaction.

In a state of afterglow,
I feel detached from my body.

I watch as Adam man-handles me
into the missionary position.

He pounces on me,
and I try to squirm away
on my haunches.

> *"Let me have what is mine!*
> *I am your master*
> *and I demand ..."*

In a seething rage,
I scream the secret name of God,
"YHWH!"
and disappear.

Darkness surrounds me.

I hear the dripping of water
and feel the cool caress of damp earth.

I left Adam in our bower
and Eden behind.

III. Fighting in Chaos

I am in a cave
carved from living rock
overlooking the Red Sea.

My utterance of the secret knowledge
propelled me out of Eden,
opening the outskirts of paradise.
I am welcomed to the realm of chaos.

Fallen creatures pay court;
I reward their advances with my body.

Ragged scratches bleed across my back,
bruises fade to maroon over my hips,
and fangs puncture my neck.

My flesh, scarred by their lust,
enjoys pain in the pursuit of pleasure.

My fertile womb fills with their ejaculate
and I birth a multitude of daemons.

My children roam by the hundreds,
traversing the world beyond Eden,
going where man has yet to see.

As the sun sinks into the horizon,
merging with the sea,
I stroll along the water's edge,
watching minnows swim in the reeds.

Glancing into the distance,
three wing'd creatures fly towards me.
The piercing light of sunset
bounces off their snowy feathers.

They drift on the rising drafts,
twirl on the breeze,
and float to the beach,
landing before me.

> "Greetings to you, Lilith,
> first of your kind,
> the All-Mother.
>
> I am Semangelof.
> These are my brothers,
> Sansenoy and Senoy.
> God sent us as envoys
> on the behalf of Adam.
>
> He has been hounded by loneliness
> and regrets his actions.
> He desires you to return."

I say confidently with a penetrating gaze.
"Although we are made of the same clay,

Adam wishes me to be his subservient wife.
I am created as an equal and a partner.
I will not serve him."

Semangelof tightens his fist.
*"If you do not come willingly,
we will be compelled to use force."*

"Do what you must
but I will not return to Adam."

They move into formation,
belligerently extending their wings
and flourishing flaming swords
as they march towards me.

As I speak the charm of making,
I wrap my hands together in a double fist
and slam the ground.

In a crackle of static and a burn of ozone,
a bubble of lightning surrounds me.

The sphere rattles with each strike.
Their swords ricochet off my barrier,
the fury of God held at bay.

Broadcasting my thoughts
into the dark realm,
I call for assistance.

From a distant growl to a rolling thunder,
the rumbling of the earth rises in volume.
My children arrive to join the fray.

As I am lifted up and away,
carried on their backs,
the angels are pulled down,
drowning in a sea of incubi.

For a fortnight, our battle rages:
With each rising sun,
one hundred of my spawn
shuffle off their mortal coil.

In the center of my brain,
I feel a vibration
as a small voice gains volume.

> *"Since we are at a stalemate,*
> *a new plan has been enacted.*
> *You are free.*

> *Call back your children.*
> *We will leave you alone*
> *in this land of twilight."*

Opening my third eye,
I project my thoughts:
Return to the darkness.

The flood of daemons recedes,
leaving the dead and the angels behind.

Semangelof turns towards me, bows,
and raises his sword in a salute.
His brothers follow suit.

They take to the air
and fly back across the sea.

Dispersing my shield of lightning,
I begin the trek back to my cave.
Overwhelmed with a great sorrow,
my vision fills with tears.

The bodies of my offspring lay around me,
mutilated and decomposing.
My freedom has come at a great price.

IV. Pillow Talk

After my arrival on these shores,
I met the archangel Samael.

We grew into lovers,
and I became his consort.

Making my way to the edge
of this carrion field,
I find him waiting for me.

He is chief of the fifth heaven,
the angel of death
and the adversary.

But on this day,
he welcomes me into his embrace,
offering me comfort in my grief
by raining the grace of God o'er me.

The first beam of morning
pierces the darkness of my cave
and crawls upon my body.

As Samael's sweat dries on my skin,
my body pulsates with orgasm's aftermath.
Our limbs entangle in a post-coitus knot.

"After you fought my brethren to a stalemate,

God put Adam into a deep slumber,
removed one of his ribs
and fashioned him a new wife,
a subservient one, Eve.

Then He lessened Adam's knowledge,
placed it into a fruit growing
on a newly sprouted tree
and declared it forbidden.

As a newly born fawn,
Eve can only learn from Adam
and her own experiences.

You contain the complete wisdom
that Adam was created with,
everything taken from him
and denied from Eve."

I swirl my fingers across his chest
and listen to his words
as they drone in my ears.

The exertions from our love-making catch up
and cause his speech to trail off,
sleep over-taking him.

Before joining him in his silent repose,
I make a resolution:

I will befriend Eve,
complete her education
and give her the ability to be free.

V. Seduction

Using a transportation spell,
I appear in a copse,
hidden from their bower.

I wait until I can meet Eve alone.
Adam heads towards the west,
meandering across an open meadow,
leaving on his daily journey.

After I'm sure he's gone,
I slip into their sleeping chamber.

Everything is put away and straightened.
The remains of their morning meal
lay near the hearth.

A splish-splash sound floats on the air
and I head towards a bubbling brook.

I catch sight of my replacement
and cloak myself in the guise of a serpent.

Sitting on a log,
I watch as she bathes.

Facing away from me,
her long hair flows down her back
in a straight rivulet, black as midnight.
Her skin glows like a pale moon.

The water creates ripples as it laps at her hips,
her curves reflecting on the mirrored surface.

As she turns towards me,
her mahogany eyes flash
and her lips glisten crimson
with an apples' juicy ripeness.

A worm of desire digs in my brain,
communicating its passion to my loins.
My nipples thicken with a rush of blood.

Adam does not deserve her.

I catch her attention
and she pauses in her movement,
slightly bewildered.

> *"We named all manner of creatures,*
> *but I do not recall seeing you."*

"Do not be afraid, my child.
I am not here to hurt you.

I offer you enlightenment
and access to secret knowledge.
I am Lilu.

What is your name?"

> *"Eve, wife of Adam...*
> *Where'd you come from?"*

"The edge of Eden
in a cave by the sea.

Come sit by me, my girl.
I think we can be friends.
Do you have any intimates?"

Taking a step towards me, she responds:
*"I have Adam and my duties.
That is enough."*

"Has he taught you about the secret pleasures?
Does he make your body tremble?
Do you forget yourself when making love?"

Her head slowly moves in a negative motion.

A handbreadth separates us.
My invisible limbs feel the heat of her skin.

"Let me open a new world for you."
Leaning forward, I press my lips onto hers.

In shock, her mouth parts,
and I slither in my tongue.
She tastes of honey.

My glamour shimmers
as I wrap my arms around her.
I enjoy the feel of her breasts on mine.

Burying my face in the crook of her neck
I deeply breathe in her hair's pine scent

and bite into the soft flesh.
A shiver runs through her body.

My lips trace her skin
and I light on a nipple,
its hardness fills my mouth.

A low moan escapes
with each of my suckles.

Gently lowering her to the straw-covered ground,
I make my way into her parted legs,
teasing her inner thigh with flicks of my tongue.

As my fingers pierce the veil of her bush,
I push through her lips and enter her chalice.
A milky liquid escapes.

Eve rides my fingers with abandon,
gyrating her hips in time to her internal rhythm.

I bring my lips to her velvet nub
and lick it with my tongue.

Her hands grab the sides of my head
and, while guiding my efforts,
holds me in place.

Her orgasmic cries echo to the clouds.
Her entire body bucks and trembles.

As she suffers the pleasure of aftershocks,
I coil myself around her.

Holding tight, I absorb her aroma.

> "This is only a sample
> of the knowledge denied you.
> You are being kept from your full potential."

"Wh—where can I go for further enlightenment?"

> "You must go to the tree
> and eat of His fruit."

"You mean the forbidden tree?"

> "Yes. Then you will be made whole."

"What about Adam?"

> "Do not worry about him.
> He lost a companion once.
> He will not again.
>
> When the time comes,
> you will know what to do.
> Now you must sleep."

As I kiss her cheek,
she closes her eyes
and drifts into a torpor.

My work is complete.
I disentangle from her body
and transport myself back to my cave
where Samael awaits me.

VI. The Fall

In a swirling torrent,
charcoal clouds spiral above Eden
as lightening sparks across the aether
followed by deafening thunder.

Uttering spoken magick
I arrive in paradise
and slither to a hiding place.

Crawling up a tree
I curl on a branch
and wait for the coming drama.

"Adam!
Where are you?"

"I am in this bush
and not fit to be seen."

"Come out so your Father may see you."

Adam steps into the clearing,
his head bowed in embarrassment
with Eve's hand held in his.

They tremble in clothing fashioned
from fig leaves and vines.

"What is this over your bodies?
Why have you covered yourselves?"

"We are naked and ashamed."

"Who told you that you were naked?"

"No one, Lord.
It is knowledge that we gained
after eating from the fruit."

"Where did you find this fruit?"

Adams eyes shift towards Eve.
"She gave it to me."

"You had every freedom here in Eden.
You could eat of every fruit
and animal except that one tree.

What drove you to disobey me?"

Eve takes a deep breath, and slowly lets it out.
"My Lord, I was shown unbelievable knowledge,
and felt more in touch with myself than I ever have.

I knew the fruit was the key to my future.
I plucked it from the tree and devoured it,
letting its juices anoint my body.

Adam came upon me as I floated in ecstasy,
took the fruit from my hand,
and shared my meal."

"Adam, did you know what fruit she ate?"

"Yes Lord,

but the thought of paradise without her
was unbearable to me.

I preferred to be damned together
than to be alone in paradise."

"Very well. So be it.
You shall leave this place
and..."

As I remove myself from my hideout
to return to my personal duties,
His words trail off and float away from me.

Reappearing in my cave
I hear the song of the earth,
through the parakeet's twitter
and the wind's whisper,
speak to me again.

"Hail Lilith!

All-Mother and Spirit of Freedom.

Unbeknownst to you,
you have served my bidding.

Humanity is placed on their destined path.

You are their Goddess,
Keeper of the moon,
and midnight secrets.

May your light burn bright upon the world."

II.

At the Gates of Ishtar

I. Coming of Age

I must take my place along the wall.
As my body transitions,
transforming from childhood
and bleeding the woman's gift,
I prepare to follow tradition.

My mother and aunt take care of me,
bathing me in rose water,
washing the dirt and grease from my hair.

The once sparkling liquid
turns an off-color grey.

I am removed from the pool,
and my nubile body is patted dry
with cloth of woven cotton.

My milky skin gains a rosy hue
as the water is whisked away
from my newly formed curves.

The ceremony of cleansing
takes place in the pure light of the moon,
its fullness representing my flowering.

I am anointed in perfumed oil,
slicking back my hair
and gleaming over my body.

Talcum is powdered,
and I am led to my bed chamber
to sleep until morning.

Upon awakening,
I eat a small breakfast of pomegranate
as my hair is brushed straight.

I am draped in a silvery silk shift,
and my head is covered with a hijab.

A carriage waits for me by the door.
A tremble radiates through my limbs
as I climb aboard.

Gazing out the window,
I watch the townspeople
go through the motions of their lives.

The baker sets fresh bread in the window to cool,
the warm wheaty scent wafting into my nostrils.

The butcher dumps a bucket of water
to clean fresh entrails from the cobbles.

The shop keeper sweeps his steps
to prepare for the day's business.

The blacksmith pounds glowing steel
while yelling at his apprentice
to pump the bellows faster.

Will I be picked by one of these men?

The gates of the temple open
and welcome me inside.

"This is your new home.

*You are obligated to stay here
until your offering is accepted.*

*Prior to this,
we will feed you,
train you and prepare you.*

*A chosen few will be granted a life of service
and become a handmaiden."*

During the first week,
we are taught to recognize
our body's wants, needs, and desires.

The meaning and power of womanhood is explored.
I learn that our pleasure must not be denied.

Under supervision
my fingertips skate over
the surface of my skin.
A slight touch brings whispers of fulfillment.

Deeper pressure and elongated fingers
discover sensual folds and a velvet nub.

I bring the glistening digits to my mouth
and wrap my tongue over their taste,
a primal musk teeming with pheromones.

Having graduated to the neophyte level,
I line up along the southern wall with the other girls:
some new like me, others unwanted and still waiting.

With a painted face and free-flowing hair,
I wait for the revelers and the lonely
to come make a selection
and worship the Goddess.

As midnight creeps into new morning,
the clear cool sky a bluish black,
I grow sleepy and consider retiring
when a middle-aged man comes to me.

With squinty eyes and a rolling stance,
he begins the ceremony:
"I invite you in the name of Mylitta."
He tosses five silver shekels at my feet.

In a nervous bow,
I bend and collect my payment.

Taking his hand in mine,
I lead him to the west wall
where the area is darkened.

A ball of exciting fear lives in my belly
as I watch him pull down his pants.

I reach forward
and grasp the hot hardness
of his pulsating manhood.

With a slight grip,
I stroke his shaft
as he moves his hips
in a gliding rhythm.

"I am ready for you."

Tugging a tie on my shoulder,
my dress flows to the ground
with a careless whisper.

I turn around and present myself to him.

He grabs my hips,
pulling me towards his body.
I feel his head searching for my opening.

There is a sharp pain
and a small pop
as he enters my crevice.
I feel liquid run down my legs.

Using my hips as handles,
he thrusts in a steady rhythm,
slapping into my buttocks.

I feel my organs shift
to accommodate his length.

His breathing sharpens
and quickly becomes ragged
as he reaches his little death.

Molten fluid fills me,
and he slumps over my back.

After sheepishly tying his pants in place,
he gives me an awkward hug
and goes on his way,
a spring in his step.

I slip back into my dress,
wander on wiggly legs
to a secret corridor,
and reenter the temple.

I show the handmaiden my bounty.

She removes two coins
and places them in her pouch.

Embracing me in a hug,
she takes me by my hand,
and leads me to the baths.

> *"You have fulfilled your obligation.*
> *You may spend the coming fortnight*
> *in pray and reflection.*
>
> *Then you must make a choice:*
> *rejoin your family and begin your life,*
> *or stay and serve the Goddess."*

II. Enlightenment

As I fly along the breeze,
I feel the intake of my daughter's breath
and the sacredness of her act.

In a gesture of self-sacrifice,
she gives her womanhood
and allows a stranger to violate her.

I am the pull of desire,
the strength of love,
the waves of war,
and the beauty of life.
It is my destiny to generate passions.

The power of their worship
calls to me across the universe,
and I spread my wisdom
to those seeking enlightenment.

III. Celebration of Akitum

The sun pierces the veil of predawn darkness
and lights up the sky in a new azure.

It is the tenth day of Akitu,
the Sumerian festival of the new year,
and the Spring Equinox.
I am the High Priestess of Inanna.

Tonight, I open my soul
and welcome Her into my being
and transform into the Goddess.

Our King will debase himself
and take on the role of a shepherd.
It is only through subjugation
that he can be elevated to Godhead.

In the temple of Eanna,
the house of heaven,
our sacred ritual will take place.

On the roof of the sky,
I am perched on my shadowy throne
and survey my domain.

The afternoon sun beats
the weary soil into submission,
causing the grasslands to shrink.

Traveling in a ball of dust,
a shepherd herds his sheep.
As he moves away from the horizon,
he looms larger in my sight.

I am intrigued.

With a wave of my hand,
I call over my handmaiden:

*"Do you see that shepherd
walking in the distance?"*

"Yes, mistress."

"Go and bring him to the temple.

*Have him bathe
and install him in my chamber.
He will dine with me tonight."*

"As you wish."

I watch as a small entourage
gallops to meet the herdsman.
His flock tries to scatter
in a nervous shuffle.

After pointing and gesturing
in a show of protest,
he relents and joins the group.

As the sun leaks under the horizon,
pulling night behind it,
various wall sconces are lit.

They lead the way down the vestibule
to where the shepherd awaits me.

Peering through the doorway,
I see him lounging on an ottoman,
casually glancing around the room.

Breathing deeply,
I walk through the entrance.

*"I am Inanna.
Welcome to my home."*

He stands as I enter
and bows with a flourish.

*"Thank you for this honor.
My name is Dumuzid."*

I gesture towards the nearby table,
and we sit together for dinner.

Hours fly by in an instant.
Our conversation covers a breadth of topics;
He is more learned than I expected.

Midnight creeps into new morning,
I lean over, skate my lips near his ear,
and sensually whisper:
"Follow me."

With a slight nibble, I saunter away.
I feel his eyes disrobe me
as they roam over my body.

I shed the layers of my clothes
until I am only covered
by a shear muslin shift.

The light radiates from various hanging lamps
causing my bare body to show through the fabric:

the darkness of my areolae,
the swell of my breast,
the curve of my hips,
and the thatch of my bush.

A wall of pillows supports me
as I lay on my bed.

My slightly parted legs
cause the hem of my shift
to hike up my thighs.

He appears in the entrance of my boudoir,
wearing nothing but his smile.

His tan body, layered in muscles, stands relaxed
with a trail of joy leading to his semi-erect penis.
I feel my skin flush at the sight of him.

With a nod of my head:
"Come to me."

His muscular majesty carries him
to the foot of my bed.
Climbing on, he crawls towards me.

I bound forward,
take his head in my hands,
and attack his lips with a soul kiss.

As our tongues explore,
I feel his hands searching my body
and then grabbing hold of my breasts.

The thin barrier of my last defense
becomes too much
and I pull it over my head.

Leaning back into my pillows
I guide him to where he is needed.

After giving my hardened nipple a taste,
his tongue traces over my belly button
and he buries himself between my legs.

I enter a fugue state as all my focus
concentrates on how he eats me.

As he laps at my chalice,
I gather bed clothes in my fists
and moan in sync to his tongue's thrusting.

In the building intensity,
I demand:
"Fuck me now!"

There is a slight lull
as he changes position
followed by his throbbing flesh
sliding into my vessel.

With each thrust,
an animal spirit shows in his face,
ferocious and wild.

I hold my legs by the knees
to give him the space he needs.

I feel his length slide in quicker thrusts
as our skin collides in sonic booms.

Letting go of my legs
I pull his face down.

Eating his lips as he ate mine,
I sense the creation of a new universe,
and a howling Big Bang explodes through my body.

His face squinches
as, with a final thrust,
he buries his cock
deep inside me.

The pulsation of liquid heat
pounds inside my velvet walls.

He slides out,
and a viscous milky liquid
coats my inner thighs.

As I bring my legs to my chest,
he wraps his body around me
and covers us in a blanket.

With our marriage bed made,
I drift into a new world,
a world of safety and contentment.

Awakening from our re-enactment,
the King looks at me and bows.

He has been humbled
and will return to his world,
leaving me to pursue Inanna.

Interlude (1)

Worship

As an aura of strength radiates,
embroidered flames on midnight silk
dance over flowing curves.

You are beauty's icon,
and the universe kneels at your feet.
The masses bestow praise and worship.

Observing your offerings,
you beckon me from the crowd,
gesturing with a sensual sway.

We stroll into your inner chamber.
As low flames light the columns,
a central dais is draped
with crimson chiffon
and feathered cushions.

At your signal,
your servants disrobe me
and anoint rose water over my skin
preparing me for the rite of spring.

I am led to a nest of pillows
and gently laid down.
A goblet of spiced wine is placed in my hand.

You appear before me:
ash blond hair crowned with woven crocus,
their royal purple reaffirming your status.

Pale fire reflects off your skin,
causing your naked torso to glow.
My eyes absorb heaven in the flesh.

As you slide your body onto me,
I feel our energy transfer
from luminous auras.

Holding your face in my hands,
I pull your lips to mine.
Our tongues dance,
and I taste your passion.

Mystical magic swirls around us
as our bodies meld into one.

At the end of our pleasures,
I encircle you with my arms
and drift towards sleep.

The morning sun awakens me,
and I find myself outside the temple walls,
a crocus flower on my chest.

My offering to the Goddess has been accepted.

III.

Woman at the Pool

I. Cleansing Ritual

With a zephyr at my back,
I approach the sacred mikvah.

The water bubbles pure, clean,
and cold from the bowels of the earth
to compose a stationary pool.

As torches offer a wavy light
in the bluish midnight darkness,
palm trees create the ambiance of an oasis.

Empty desert stars stare at me
as they loom over the roof
of the darkened palace.

It has been a week since
the bloom of my scarlet flower wilted;
I must purify myself.

Standing on the edge of the bath,
I peer into the sky
and think about my ancestors:

Women of inner strength that stretch
to the beginning of known time
who, living under the rule of men,
carved out their own place.

With a practiced movement,
my hands follow their own mind

and untie my robe.
I let it slip to the sandy pavers.

As the caress of the wind
causes my skin to dimple
and my nipples to harden,
I step into the water.

After inhaling a deep breath, I submerge myself.
The quietude of the womb presses upon me.

I rub my hands over my body
and imagine the calloused ones of Uriah.
I love how he touches me;
It is lonely being a soldier's wife.

In a moment of inspiration,
I plant my feet firmly on the pool's bottom
and explode through the water's surface.
The sound of droplets splash around me.

Feeling free and exhilarated,
I scoop up my drapings
and slide into them.

The dry cloth sticks
to the wetness of my body
and outlines my form.

Satisfied with the completed ritual,
I make my way home to my empty house.
I pray for my husband's safe return...

II. The Summoning

Deep in the bowels of my home
while completing my daily chores,
I hear a heavy-fisted knock
pound on my door.

With a dragging creak,
I open the front entrance
and see two kingsmen
standing at a relaxed rest.

> *"What causes the noble guard*
> *to darken my doorway?"*

"We seek Bathsheba, the daughter of Eliam.
Does she reside at this residence?"

> *"It is me you seek."*

"The king requests you to join him for an audience.
Will you accompany us?"

> *"I am a loyal subject*
> *and will do as I am bid."*

Excited with the thrill of a summons
I follow the king's guard
and make my way to the palace.

III. An Audience with the King

The palace steward ushers me
into a large room with draping silks
flowing from the walls to the ceiling.

Sunlight streams through an open balcony,
causing the cloth colors to appear translucent.

Lucious pillows are piled on a central mat.

On a side-table, fruits and sweetmeats
lay out in a tantalizing display.
Their succulent aroma drifts to my nose.

"Taste whatever you like."

I turn towards the voice,
and gaze upon the king.

"Forgive me, my lord,"
I say and fall to my knees in homage.

"No. No. Please don't do that.
I invited you here as my guest.
Allow me to help you stand."

I take his outstretched support
and regain my feet.
I feel the strength of his grip
and the roughness of his palm.

"I wish to speak with you.
Please sit with me."

"*Yes, my lord.*"

As we nestle among the pillows,
his eyes dart around
as if he cannot look at me.

"It was three nights before now
that I felt restless within these walls
[he gestures around the room]
and made my way to the roof.

The cool night breeze usually helps to calm my mind,
but on this night, my inner passion became inflamed.

What do you think I saw?"

Since I'm not sure he wants an answer,
I shrug my shoulders and give a questioning glance.

"I looked over the palace walls
towards a group of palm trees.
Their fluttering torch flames drew me
like a wayward moth.

The grove stood guard over a shimmering
mirror reflecting the mysteries above it.
The scintillating stars doubled before me.

Like a butterfly emerging from its cocoon,

an angelic vision stepped from her robe
and slowly descended into the pool.
The curves of her body transported me.

I lost sight of her as she
submerged beneath the surface.

With a forceful explosion,
she reappeared with a watery mist
glowing around her.

The intensity of her magnificence
took my breath away
and burned my retinas.

I immediately sent envoys to inquire,
and now I find you before me
even more radiant than I beheld."

As he speaks these final words,
his hand moves up my covered thigh.

A feeling of shocked numbness
mixed with excitement
courses through my system.

He takes my lack of protest as consent
and advances his conquest.

As he leans into me,
scented oils penetrate my olfactory sense.

His lips are soft in the bristles of his beard.
I close my eyes and imagine kissing Uriah.

A squeezing pressure holds my breast.
His fingers tweak my nipple through the fabric
and coax my blood to flow into hardness.

As my pent-up sexual energy unties itself,
I decide to ignore my marriage vows
and unleash my desire upon my aggressor.

With my hand over his,
I push it harder into my chest.
Pleasure pulses along with my heartbeat.

My tongue invades his mouth,
and I can taste the sweetness of his breath
imbued with a tinge of mint.

My free hand drifts towards his stomach,
blindly traces below his bellybutton,
and discovers the king's scepter,
hot like freshly molten gold.

With a slip of my hand, I free his mandrake.
A greedy moan screams past his lips
as I trace from his root to his head
in a fondling motion.

I time the thrusts of my tongue
with the stroking of his member.

The tender flesh of my inner palm
burns with his throbbing heat.

To the king's disappointment,
I stop abruptly and stand up,
but he cannot speak due
to the lack of blood in his brain.

I take three steps away, turn around,
and let my clothes slip off my body.

I see the fine hairs on my skin glow from
the light coming from behind me.

"My lord king remove your finery!"

In a flurry of movement,
he rushes to meet my demand.

I saunter over,
out-stretch my index finger,
and push him into a supine position.

I take a moment to enjoy the scenery:
a muscular field that is his body
with a lone oak standing at attention.

The end of my extended hand
traces over his skin,
leaving a path of goose bumps.

My womanhood yearns
for the joining of our flesh.

I squat over him
and use my hand
to guide his mass.

With my legs and thighs,
I control the speed at which
his length travels my corridor.

I close my eyes
and savor the firing
of my pleasure zones.

He grows harder as I grip tighter.

Pressure builds inside me,
and I use his chest for support,
clawing my mark into his skin.

"Pinch my nipples!"

My hips buck like an Arabian stallion,
causing our slapping flesh
to echo throughout the room.

My sense of self focuses
on the cock ramming inside me,
pushing my mind to the universal truth.

We implode together
as his fluid fire fills my reservoir.

For a micron of time,
I transcend the mundane
and feel God burn through me.

I collapse in a sweaty ball
and roll off the king exhausted
from my expenditure of energy.

"Hold me."

As I lay there feeling the comfort
of his arms wrapped around me,
the liquid of life leaks down my thigh
and puddles on the cushions.

IV. The Aftermath

I awaken in the darkened hideaway
with a chill radiating over my body.
The king left the ghost of his warmth beside me.

After quickly dressing and putting myself together,
the waiting steward leads me out of the palace.

Since my journey in the mid-morning,
the streets have become cloaked
in the dawn of twilight.

With torches and oil lamps wicking into life,
I re-examine my royal encounter.

The primal energy of our union
still pulses through my loins.
I feel his hands over my body
and the caress of his lips.

I love the headiness of my essence
cresting on the wave of orgasm,
a relentless pounding of water on sand.

In between the remembrance of pleasure,
an angry pulsing reveals itself deep in my psyche,
red and impotent with the outrage of being cornered.

The inner fury and past passion
blend in equal parts
magnifying my senses.

The murmur of the street roars
as the scent of seared meat overpowers.

The smoothness of my clothes' caress
reminds me of the king's touch.

I fall to my knees,
hold my head with my hands,
and voice a silent howl
to force the cacophony
of input to subside.

After mending my fractured feelings,
I drift along the rest of my journey
and make my way home.

As I enter, I glance to the wall
and see items of Uriah
awaiting his return.

The realization of my betrayal
floods through my system,
and a cloud of guilt descends.

I rend my clothes
and dive towards
the cold fire pit.

I grab fistfuls of burnt wood dust
and powder my sinful skin
by smearing ash into my face
and rubbing ash into my hair.

I must make my inward disgust visible.

Streaks of tears
burrow through the grayness
and leave a clean path on my cheeks.

As upset waves cycle through my body,
my throat swells with raw anguish.
I curl into a ball and let exhaustion take over.

V. Delicate Situation

With the days progressing into weeks,
I detach myself from the event
and block the looming black guilt.

But there is a nagging pull
in the back of my brain
which will not allow me to forget.

This feeling courses through my body
which reshapes it for a new function.

My swelling breasts
cause my nipples
to throb with a soreness.

Waves of nausea attack my stomach
as, at the same time, I crave strange food.

After the time of my monthly gift passes
without its regular occurrence,
I go to my mother and seek her guidance.

I answer her questions
and let her make her examination.

The seed of the king has taken hold
and grows inside me.

VI. Second Summoning

After my time of mourning,
a litter with colorful gauze curtains
and bilious satin pillows appears at my door.

Accompanied by guards
and resting on the shoulders of eight men,
the transport is lowered to the ground for my access.

✧✧✧✧✧

When I realized my condition,
I sent a letter to the king
to inform him of his upcoming fatherhood.

Since much time passed,
I thought he was willfully ignoring me.

Then the shock of Uriah's death
nearly drove me to my own.
That is the danger of being a soldier's wife.

Although the great sorrow
and sense of abandonment crushed me,
the life growing in my womb
gave me the strength to continue.

Every day, I awoke,
and the darkness slipped
further behind.

With each measured step the city glides past,
the stride of my bearers is smooth and consistent.
The king's subjects gawk.

We pass through the gates of the palace
and into the courtyard
where the familiar steward meets us.

He bows before me,
his nose almost touching the ground.

Upon returning to an up-right position,
he beckons me with a wave of his hand
and guides me into the throne room.

The echo of my steps bounces
from the walls and to my ears.

I spy his wives scattered throughout
and the seat of power empty before me.

As David flows into the room,
I instantly go to my knees,
and tremble with a bowed head.

Squeezing my eyes tight,
I wait for an action or a word.
What is to be my fate?

I hear the shuffle of his feet as he walks over,
the weight of his presence hovering.

He kneels beside me, leans his mouth
to the edge of my ear, and whispers.

"I have brought you here to become my wife.
Will you join my family?"

Relief spills down my cheeks
and waters the tiles with loud splashes.

> *"Yes.*
> *Thank you, my lord."*

As he stands,
he wraps me in his arms
and pulls me to my feet.

"She said, 'Yes!'
Let us commence the ceremony
and begin the celebration
of this joyous occasion!"

My sister wives come around
and swoop me away into the next room
where I am draped in regalia
and anointed with oils.

The afternoon is a whirlwind
of juxtaposed images, music, and dancing.

VII. A Joyous Occurrence Reversed

The midwife crouches between my spread legs
waiting for the emergence of my child.

With each session of pushing,
sweat beads form up on my brow
and veins protrude on my neck.
I hold the bed clothes in clinched fists.

The rumblings of a primal yell
boil from my diaphragm
in sync with my maternal straining.

After ten hours of labor,
I want this being out of my body.

Gathering my resolve,
I ready myself for a final push
timed with the crest of my pain-wave.

Bearing down forcefully,
I scream away the agony
and feel the world lighten
in a liquid rush.

My handmaidens scoop up
a bloody bundle of a little being
and frantically work to clear its breathing passage.

The slow seconds drift by
in an eternal silence before finally,
with the slap of a hand,
the first breath is followed
by a hearty cry.

My baby is born,
and I have delivered a son,
an heir for David.

After a few days,
a severe illness struck,
his little body burning in the fire of fever.

I can only watch as he writhes
in a pain that he does not understand.
His cries pierce my ears.

David will not come to see him.

I pray for God to bring relief
and end the enormous agony
coursing through his tiny body.

It is almost a blessing when
the Lord finally takes him from us
and ends his suffering with a calm peace.

David will not even name him.

In the face of this tragedy,
I am hollow and invisible.

As I sit in a mourning vigil,
I overhear Nathan speak to my husband.

"...must accept this death as God's sign,
condemning the adulterous passions
that led to his birth. Not only that, but you sent
a man to his death to take his wife..."

I do not hear David's mumbled answer.
I broke my previous marriage vow
and this death is payment for that sin.

My little son lies here wrapped in black swaddling.
Beautiful in a peaceful repose.

Tomorrow is the burial.
Tomorrow I will cry and wail.
Tomorrow...

VIII. Another Chance

Soon after the death of my unnamed son,
the passion of our first encounter is
supplanted with a shared loss.

I learned that David fasted
and spent nights wearing sackcloth
while sleeping on the ground
to plead with God to spare our child.

We join together
in the search of comfort
and plant a seed.

I am rewarded
with the birth
of a healthy child.

We travel to the temple
to see the Prophet Nathan.

He declares Solomon as Jedidiah,
beloved of the Lord.

IX. Passing of the Torch

As the lust and vigor of youth
succumbs to the frailties of old age,
David becomes disenchanted with life
and loses control of his eldest born.

It comes to pass that Adonijah,
the oldest surviving fourth son,
declares himself king
and set about a celebration.

News of this event whispers around the kingdom
until it lands in the ears of the uninvited.

After meeting with Nathan,
it is decided that David must be reminded
of Solomon's destined birthright.

I enter the sick room
and see David laying
propped on pillows.

"My lord.
You are here,
the rightful ruler of Israel,
but Adonijah has said
that he is king and the heir."

Nathan enters and takes up the argument.

"Yes. I have heard the same.
In fact, your son, at this moment,
celebrates his coronation
with a great feast excluding
everyone who would say otherwise.

What shall we do?"

David stretches his arms wide
as if giving a benediction.

"On this very night,
I anoint Solomon
in the sacred oil of Kingship.

I declare him my heir
and king of the land!"

Envoys quickly dispatch
to spread the news to the people
and end the false celebration.

X. Intercessor to the King

Solomon grows into his wisdom and his birthright,
with me acting as his intercessor.
I deliver petitions unto the king.

When I enter the room,
my son rises to meet me.
He bows in veneration
honoring me as Queen Mother.

After taking me by the hand,
he guides me to the seat at his right.
The murmurs of those waiting cease
and court commences.

IV.

Most Beloved

I. Demons Begone!

As I writhe in the dusty road
with a small dirt cloud floating around me,
a cloak of terror drowns my consciousness.

My teeth clack together with quick chomps
as frothy foam bubbles seep through my lips.
"Put this stick in her mouth.
Don't let her bite off her tongue."

The world's vibration slows
as I stare through fluttering lids.

An oily high-pitched sound
snakes between my hemispheres.
Distinct voices whisper behind my brain:

"She's mine! I claim her by right."
"See the way she squirms!"
"Suck upon her soul, and feast on eternity."

A pair of cool palms caress my face,
their thumbs pushing pressure into my forehead.

"In the name of the hosts in heaven
and the power of my Father,
whose words spake and brought life,
I command thee and bring you to obedience!"

My limbs go straight as boards,
and the enemy in my mind goes silent.

"Exit from this woman of grace
and leave her body as her own!"

My flesh goes flush
as fluid drains into my stomach.
Bile and gore rushes up my throat
and evacuates with a splat.

Raising my head, I barely glance
and see creatures squirming in the muck
before falling back to the ground.

"I have removed the demons.

You there.
Bring her inside.
Let her regain her strength."

I hear the stranger take his leave.
As I'm being lifted, I whisper,
"Who is that who saved me?"

"He is Yeshua, the son of a carpenter.
Enough questions. You must rest."

With the taste of his name upon my lips,
I drift into a peaceful stupor.

II. Becoming One Flesh

Yeshua's lips tickle my ear
and caress my forehead
before planting themselves
firmly on mine.

His breath escapes,
and I breathe the vapor
of his Godhead.

With a resolute placement of his hands,
he reminds me that I am his most beloved—
the one he holds in esteem over
Peter and the others.

My breasts throb in time
with the rhythm of his fingers
and their grappling strength.

Soon after he drove the demons from me,
I left my familial home in Magdala
and followed him.

I take care of his earthly needs,
and those of his disciples,
to further the spread of his message.

I live with the knowledge
that I must share him
with the world and his Father.

He shares the Word with me,
and I know that it is good.
I long for the coming of his kingdom.

He is without a throne and its accoutrements,
but with a smooth fumbling of my hands,
I bring his scepter to its full attention.

I push him onto his back,
and my hips hover over his.
My velvet sheath glistens with anticipation.

I caress the root of his saber
and guide his throbbing mass
into the safety of my cave.

A rotating rhythm courses through my body
as the fire of our loins intermingle.

His hands wrap around my waist
and regulate the motion.

I complete our circuit
by putting my mouth upon his,
and suck his tongue in a mirrored tempo.

We elevate deep into our joined psyche
as the world around us disappears.

Our universe begins anew
with the implosion of a Big Bang
drowning us in waves of ecstasy.

I slump into his chest,
let his arms wrap around me,
and drift on the wash of our love.

III. Stations of the Cross

As I stand in this place of skulls
watching Yeshua's excruciation,
I hold his mother in my arms,
letting my mind drift to the recent past.

When we had broken bread during Passover,
a sense of foreboding hovered over us
like a thick fog embracing the ground.

In honor of my status among the disciples,
I am a seated at his right hand.

He spoke of a betrayal,
a thrice denial,
and fed us his body and blood
in remembrance of him.

With the placing of the
unleavened disc on my tongue,
he entered my body for a final time.
The offered wine cleansed my pallet as I swallowed.

Our last supper closed
with the bestowing
of a final commandment:

*To love one another
as I have loved you.*

After the kiss of Judas
and the arrest in the garden,
we scattered and hid lest we be taken too.

Throughout the night, murmurs and gossip
kept us informed of the progress of his trial.

Driven by my need to do something
and tired of huddling in fear,
I followed the rising sun
and made my way to Herod's palace.

As I approached,
the crowd thundered:

*"Barabbas!
Give us Barabbas!
We want Barabbas!"*

While washing his hands in a bowl,
the Prefect Pilate said:

"So be it.

Let Yeshua's blood
rest on your hands,
for I am innocent."

With a wave,
he motioned for Yeshua
to be bound to a pillar.

The high whine of a whip
sliced repeatedly through the air,
accented by a fleshy pop!
Grunts of anguish echoed through us.

I could not look away…

A soldier walked out
of a darkened alcove
with a woven halo.

"If you are king of the Jews,
you need a crown.
We made you one of thorns!"

The small spikes caused gleaming
blood to stream down his face.
He held a stoic gaze over the crowd.

He was then dragged by his chain
to where a wooden beam waited for him.

"Here is your throne.
You must transport it
to the place of your punishment."

Soldiers lifted the beam
and settled it upon his shoulder.
Although his knees quivered,
he stayed upright.

The crowd split like the Red Sea
to form a path towards his destination.

As I watched him shuffle along,
I wanted to rend my clothing
and put an end to the madness,
but I knew this must take place.

Yeshua's entire body trembled
and he collapsed into a pile.
The rood rolled off his back.

His mother, Miriam, floated
out of the sea of people.

She stood looking into his eyes
and rested her hand on his cheek
where it became soiled
with his sweat and blood.

I watched him gain strength
from her presence and recover.

A soldier grabbed a man
and dragged him into the road,
"You will help carry his burden."

I went to Miriam
and put my arm
around her shoulder.

"Let me support you
as his teachings
have supported us."

Together we traveled behind him
and used our will to complete his journey.

Before making it to the Golgotha,
a woman, using a finely woven cloth,
wiped the sweat and grime from his face.

He collapsed twice more,
only to regain his feet,
and continue his progression.

After cresting the hill,
I saw an empty space between two other prisoners
who had been installed on their beams.

The crossbar was taken from the conscripted man,
and Yeshua was laid on his wooden bed
with his arms spread wide.

Howls of agony punctuated each hammer-strike
as spikes pierced his wrists and ankles.

After hauling the cross to its upright position,
the soldiers threw dice to claim
ownership over his clothing.

I snap out of my reverie
as I hear Yeshua draw a deep breath.

He looks towards the sky,
and calls out:

*"My God, my God,
why have you forsaken me?"*

Black clouds swirl over us
blotting out the afternoon sun.
The heaviness of black midnight
oppresses our souls.

Wind whips around
and pulls at our clothing.

Dropping his eyes from heaven,
a faint whisper leaks from his lips:
"It is finished."

His head droops
as his body goes slack
with only the spikes holding him upright.

IV. Glorious Reunion

In the predawn darkness,
I walk with my companions to Yeshua's tomb
along a path that winds through desolate rock.

Since sundown of Sabbath
happened soon after his death,
we had to bury him quickly.
We now need to finish anointing his body.

A shiver vibrates through my spine:
The stone is rolled away from the tomb's entrance.

All it takes is a brief glance inside
to know he is gone.

In a hurried frenzy,
I run back along our path
and come upon Peter.

"Yeshua's tomb is open,
and his body is nowhere
to be found!"

Peter calls upon John to join us,
and we explore the tomb,
where we find linen left in a bodily shape.

As a gusher of grief wells in my soul
from the compounded loss,
I stay behind as the others vacate the area.

I throw myself into the dirt
and let my sadness overtake me.

Through a blurry lens of tears,
I look through the tomb's entrance
and see two wing'd creatures in blazing white.

"Why are you distraught and crying?"

I respond with a defiant posture:
*"My lord's body has been taken,
and I do not know where he's been laid."*

I sense motion from the corner of my eye
and turn to face who has disturbed me.
A stranger stands before me.

*"Woman, why are you weeping?
Whom are you looking for?"*

*"Sir. Have you taken my beloved from his tomb?
Tell me where he has been laid,
and I will take possession of my duty."*

As the stranger's mouth forms my name,
I recognize him for his true self,
and outstretch my arms towards him.

"Yeshua!"

He holds a splayed hand towards me.
"Nay! You mustn't hold onto me.
I have not yet joined with my Father.

Go to our brothers, and tell them
'I am ascending to my Father and your Father,
to my God and your God.'

The time has arrived for you to spread
the Word about the arrival of my Kingdom."

With flush cheeks, I smile at him.
"As you wish, my beloved."

After turning to leave, I look back.
The tomb is empty as if no one had been there…

Interlude (II)

Mystic Fusion

𝕴 stroll through a stone arch
and enter the temple with a bowed head.
The time of worship has arrived.

Sitting in a pew
across from the altar,
I watch as a candle flame flickers.

You flow into the room
and move with a muscular harmony,
honed through sweat and toil.

Intelligence radiates from your golden gaze,
piercing my psyche with its fire.

You take my hand
and lead me to your chamber.
I enfold you in my arms
and am pulled by eternity.

Being near you is transcending,
but I always have an internal tremble
like a freshly born colt standing
for the first time.

As the strumming of a lute begins,
you seat me on a sofa
and sensually shed white lace
channeling Aphrodite.

My eyes follow the curve of your hips,
hover over your stomach,
and glance at your breasts.
Nipples invite me to suckle.

I contemplate your oval face,
and wonderfully full lips
framed by flaxen hair.

You lean into me.
Your perfume fills my nostrils,
pheromones amplify emotions.

As your parted mouth covers mine,
our tongues dance in a soul kiss,
and I breathe deeply of your essence.

You rip off my clothing,
throw it on the floor,
and, with a gentle push,
lay me on my back.

As you cover me like a blanket,
our skins' warmth intermingles,
and I feel your heartbeat.

Gravity pulls us together,
and you meld into me.
Our bodies fuse as one.

I feel your blood in my veins,
your air in my lungs,
and your thoughts in my mind.
Our hearts are together.

In a hermaphroditic state,
we explore our new self.

As blood gorges,
and expands our organs,
tingling skin becomes flush.

With a light touch,
we trace a hidden crevice,
teasing ourselves.

Our flesh becomes hard and erect.

Pleasure courses through our body.
radiating from our groin,
over our chest,
and into our head.

In our intertwined mind,
every secret thought and desire
becomes shared knowledge.

Rushing headlong,
our body reaches a crescendo,
and a climax trembles over our limbs.

An orgasmic wave washes us.

Exhaustion rolls over,
and we collapse into a deep sleep.

In the black of night,
with all the candles snuffed,
I awaken.

During our slumber,
we disentangle,
and I am my separate self again.

There is no sign of you,
but you have left your mark,
my spirit transformed and full of love.

V.

Innocence Unfound

I. Arrest on Terra Mater

The blizzard of apple blossoms
springs from my trees
and fills the air with
a fragrant scent.

I stroll through my orchard
while wearing my favorite
red paragon bodice
and commune with nature.

The tips of my fingers
explores the roughness of their bark,
searching for areas of concern.

I feel Gaia vibrate her
words through the wood.
"They are coming for you."

The pounding of horse hooves
gallops through the woods.

With a fluid motion,
the head magistrate
dismounts from his steed
and comes towards me.

His compatriots watch
and wait for potential trouble.

"You have been accused of witchcraft.
Please accompany us to the Village
where we will sort out this matter to its conclusion."

I know it futile to resist,
so I make my way towards
the riderless horse.

"There is no need to bind my hands.
I come with you freely.
Pray help me mount this beast."

With the orchard receding behind me,
the scent of apple blossoms wafts from my clothing
along the breeze created by the horse's canter.

II. The Interrogation

With my accusers sitting along a wall,
I enter the examination room.
My hands loosely bound in hemp.

The power of my inner magnetism
overcomes their motor controls:
Each one convulses and drools
when I move towards them.

After I find my seat, I hear the following:
"Bridget Bishop you are now brought
before Authority to give account
of what witchcrafts you are conversant in.

I take all these people
as witness to the charges."

With a dramatic flourish,
the examiner speaks to the afflicted.

"Hath this woman hurt you?"
I watch as the women
along the wall affirm this question.

"You are hereby accused
by these women for hurting them.
What do you say to it?"

I stare at him with a blank look.
"I never saw these persons before,
nor was I ever in this place before."

"They say you bewitched
your first husband to death."

"If it pleases your worship,
I know nothing of it."

"It has been affirmed that you have been
accounted as a witch these past 10 years."

"I am no witch."

"What contract have you
made with the Devil?

It has been told that you have wrote in his book,
and have tried to have others do the same."

"I have no familiarity with the devil."

"How is it then
that your appearance
doth hurt these?"

"I know not for I am innocent."

"You seem to practice witchcraft
before us by the motion of your body.
Watch as you have influence upon the afflicted."

"I know nothing of it.
I am innocent of being a witch.
I know not what a witch is."

"How do you know then
that you are not a witch?"

"I do not know what you say."

"How can you know you are no witch
and yet not know what a witch is?"

"I am clear:
If I were any such person,
you should know it.

You may threaten,
but you can do no more
than you are permitted.

I am innocent of being a witch."

"What do you say of those murders
you are charged with?"

"I hope I am not guilty of murder."

"It may be that you do not know.
Others, who have been examined before you,
have confessed today that they are witches."

"No. I know nothing of it."

Two men stand in open court
and affirm that they had told me.

"Why look you,
now you are taken
in a flat lie."

"I did not hear them."

"Does it not trouble you
to see these afflicted persons
so tormented?"

"I am not troubled for them
as I am innocent
and have done no ill."

"Do you think these unfortunates
have been bewitched?"

"I cannot tell what to think of them."

"We have heard enough.
Please take Mrs. Bishop away,
and we will deliberate."

The bailiff makes me stand
by tugging on my hemp binding,
and leads me out of the room.

✧✧✧✧✧

As I sit in my cell,
staring at the ceiling
and contemplating my fate,
the sneaking voice of gossip finds my ear.

The whispering echoes to me:
*"She has been found complicit in witchcraft,
and will have to answer to the charges."*

III. Bodily Invasion

Kneeling on the floor
with my hands folded before me,
I lean over my bed in prayer.

"Let them stop this madness.
Let them find me innocent.
Let them release me."

I feel my spirit rise out of my body
and commune with a greater force.

The rattling of my cell door
tumbles me back to the mundane.

Two women rush into the room,
grapple me with their hands,
and drag me into the hallway.

After shoving me into a wall,
the ladies peel away the layers of my clothes
and leave me as I came into the world.

A gauntlet of grabbing hands and probing fingers
becomes detached from the faces I recognize,
exploring every hill and crevice of my body.

Each breast is lifted
with my nipples being tweaked.

Hands caress my buttocks
with fingers exploring its hole.

My lips are pulled from my gums,
as I roll out my tongue for it to be held.

The fat of my belly is squeezed.

The cleft of my womanhood
is tried for true with spittle-coated digits.

My skin burns red
with the blood of shame.
I feel dirty and used.

A male baritone asks,
*"Have you found any
marks of the witch?"*

*"Yes, Doctor Barton.
We found a hidden skin growth."*

*"That is well and good.
Return her to her cell."*

Without allowing me to cover my nakedness,
I am unceremoniously tossed onto my bed.
My stripped clothing follows
and lands in a pile on the floor.

As the door slams with a creak,
I hear the twitter of voices float away
in search of their next conquest.

IV. The Verdict

The verdict has been read,
and I'm not surprised at the outcome.

My trial began in the morning,
and I sat before seven judges.

The "evidence" compiled over the preceding weeks
was presented in a logical concise manner
that explained my guilt.

I did not realize how much the local village hated me.
If I had been allowed counsel to argue a defense,
I might have had a chance to prove my innocence.

I feel numb and detached.

V. End of the Rope

As I'm led into the outdoors,
my vision takes on a heightened awareness.

The blue of the sky flows over the horizon
and puddles with splashes of yellow sun.

The green of the grass forms
from these intermingled colors
and glows with an inner light.

I follow the trunk of a red maple
and skate along the roots
into the moistness of the soil.

I sense the teeming of microscopic life
burrowing through the aerated mulch.
I taste the freshness of nature's scent.

"Come along now.
We mustn't keep 'em waitin'."

My focus narrows from its all-encompassing view,
and I see the crowd before me.
No one will make eye contact.
Unlike my guilt, theirs is real.

I am taken by the hand
and, as a cavalier helps his lady,
I am assisted onto an elevated platform.

A swaying noose dangles from a beam.

*"Do you have any last words?
Do you repent of being a witch?"*

I tighten my lips into a thin line
and move my head in a negative motion.

"Proceed with the court's judgement!"

The rope is lowered
and my neck is threaded
through the loop.

The large knot is tightened
at the base of my skull.

At the count of

3...

    2...

        1...

the support of the platform
falls from under my feet.

I plummet through the air,
and the rope loop tightens
with a CRACK!

My vision goes black.

My bladder lets go.
My body gyrates in death's rattle.

I feel the caress of a loving hug
lift me from my dying flesh.

"Daughter, come with me.
You are under my protection."

VI.

Angel of Assassination

I. Prologue to Action

𝕴 travel along the road from my cousin's estate
with the weight of summer heat collapsing upon me.
It pushes the air from my lungs.

As the closeness of Paris replaces
the green openness of the countryside,
I acquire a room at the Hôtel de Providence.

I support the Revolution.
I support the fall of monarchy.
I support the rights of man.

But, as the radical fractions took over,
things turned bloody with the September Massacres.

The earth became a muddy red mass
as over a thousand prisoners were exterminated.

And, finally, in January of this year,
King Louis XVI… executed.

The writings of Jean-Paul Marat
paved the way for these atrocities.

He stirs men's hearts to violence.
For the Republic to survive,
he must be stopped.

II. Tool of the Trade

The top of the blade catches my eye
as it gleams in a sunbeam.
It calls me to pick it up.

The weight balances well
as I curl my fingers
around the wooden hilt.

The energy of death flows
through this common kitchen knife.
I have found the implement I need.

III. The Path Diverges

To warn others who dare trod the same path,
I intended to make a grand spectacle of his murder
by preforming the act in front of the Nat'l Convention.

But that was not to be.
Marat stopped attending these meetings
due to his deteriorating health.

I must devise a new course of action…

IV. Embracing the Call of History

$\mathfrak{J}$ust before the sun reaches its daily pinnacle,
I take in a deep breath and knock on his door.

After being opened,
a stooped servant asks,
"What may we do for you?"

*"I need to speak with Monsieur Marat.
I have information concerning
a planned Girondist uprising in Caen."*

"Please wait here."

She leaves the door slightly ajar,
and goes back into the house to inquire.

After some few minutes,
the door reopens
and the sister of his fiancée
darkens the entrance.

*"Please leave.
He is not here to speak with you."*

So as not to draw attention,
I do as she asks
and make my exit.

I watch as the sun leaks from the sky
and wait for evening to darken
before knocking on Marat's door again.

He opens his entrance,
and after a quick discussion,
admits me into his house.

"Please excuse me.
I don't mean be unseemly,
but resting in a tub of water
is the only way I can bear my condition."

He slips out of his robe,
drapes it over a chair,
and slides into a bath of calm water.

"What can you tell me of this Girondist plot?"

As I spew the names he craves to hear,
he immediately jots the pertinent information.

While his attention is focused on his work,
he does not notice as I draw the blade
from the inner fold of my skirt.

With the wooden handle firmly in my grip,
the knife becomes an extension of my arm.

118

Using a hidden strength, I lunge forward
and plunge the implement into his chest.

I watch his flesh part
as the steely edge travels
through a pair of ribs.

The final rhythm of his heart
vibrates through the metal.
My heartbeat mirrors his.

As his life seeps into the still water, he calls out,
"*Aidez-moi, ma chère amie!*"
("Help me, my dear friend!")
and dies flowing over the edge of the tub.

V. Fallout

I let go of the embedded knife
as a clatter of feet rush into the room.
Arms wrap around me and shove me into a wall.

I watch his fiancée's face drain of life
as her eyes intermingle with the scene.

Marat is dragged from the tub
and onto the floor in an effort to revive him.
A flood of inert bathwater rolls over my feet.

As word spreads about my actions,
faceless officials arrive to bombard me with questions,
and to calm the hysterical crowd.

"Did you act alone?"
"Who did you conspire with?"
"Do you know what you've done?"

"Give her to us!"
"She is a traitor to France!"
"I have a rope to crack her neck!"

The hand of fate guided me and made my aim true.
I am at peace with the direction of my decisions.

VI. Final Judgement

Standing alone in the tumbril,
I listen to the circular creak of the wooden wheels
as the oxen pulls me through the crowd.

They welcome me with lustful jeers
while raining rotten vegetables upon my head.
The great unwashed love an execution…

A passing summer shower
drowns me in its sorrows.

The cheap fabric of my red overblouse
bleeds color onto my off-white clothing
while molding them to the form of my curves.

The courts declared me to be a traitor
without realizing my actions were for the Republic.

To prepare for my final act,
my hair is shorn short
to leave my neck unencumbered.

The erect majesty of the guillotine grows larger
with its blade and wooden trellis stained a pale pink.
A murder of crows watches my approach.

After reaching my destination,
I am led out of the cart.

The power of the earth flows
from the mud into my bare feet
to lessen the tremble of my legs.

I am not afraid.
I pray for my soul to be received
into the bosom of the greater power.

After the removal of my bonnet,
I am strapped onto a board, lifted prone,
and slid forward between the legs of the guillotine.

I feel the weight of the blade
float above my head.
I live for an eternity as I wait.

CLICK!

    ZOOM!

        CLUNK!

VII. Last Words

𝕴 open my eyes in the basket's semi-darkness
as light leaks through woven seams.

Searing pain courses across my neck
and my detached body registers numb.
Fingers curl through my hair, make a fist,
and yank me into the open air.

With a pendulum sway, I oscillate,
dripping blood in a splatter pattern.

A blurry figure holds me at arm's length
and with his free hand slaps my cheek.
Through broken capillaries, a blush spreads.

As my consciousness
lets go of my carcass,
I must impart a message.

I pull in humid air
through my torn trachea
with the sky becoming my lungs.

In a staccato rush,
words escape my mouth:

"I killed one man…
…to save…
…a hundred thousand."

Interlude (III)

Rite of Spring

Take my hand
and step with me
into the circle.

I am the great god Pan,
and you are my nymph.

The time has arrived
to release our inhibitions
and celebrate debauchery.

We are the sacrifice
for the rite of Spring.

Let us commit
to the celebration of flesh
and defile our temples.

Can you feel their eyes upon us?

Do not be afraid.
We are already undressed
in their imagination.

This stage is our shady bower,
a place of secret seduction.

I take you in my arms
and hold you close.

The scent of your hair
wafts into my nose:
lilac with a hint of rosemary.

I hug you tight to contain
the nervous tremble
of your beating heart.

With a twist of my head,
I bring my lips in contact with yours.
The Ley line's power
courses through your body.

Your tongue flickers into my mouth
and I taste your essence.
I close my eyes in abandon.

I pull a ribbon
and free you from the entanglement
of your white linen shift.

It puddles to your feet
in a silent whisper.

I gaze in awe at your curves.

The swell of your breast
and shape of your hips
deepens my desire.

After stepping out of my pants
and slipping my shirt over my head,
I kneel before you.

A crimson blush flowers
as I lean forward and kiss your belly.
I outline your thigh with my tongue
and savor your salty, musky taste.

I sit with my legs before me
my manhood ready to connect.

Using my shoulders to steady yourself,
you slowly lower your port upon me.
Your nether lips slide over my shaft.
I feel a tight heat.

You settle into my lap,
wrap your arms around me,
and give my soul a kiss.

Elemental magick flows through us
with the rise and fall of your hips.

Our gaze locks
as the universe opens above.

With pleasure's pressure building,
we levitate into the air.

Our breath flows together
in sync with your expanded rhythm.
Your gliding chalice grips me.

As we near the end of our sensual journey,
the hands of the Goddess reaches to cradle us.

Your bucking body causes moans to escape
from both our mouths as we find our climax.

We melt into each other,
puddle onto the floor,
and end the ritual.

The coven swarms over us
and celebrates the welcoming of Spring.

VII.

So...

You Want to Be in Movies

I. The Great Picture Show

Ever since my father first brought me,
the cinema became my true religion,
and I've been a faithful follower.

The actors were akin to gods.
That was the only way my child brain
could conceive their larger-than-life reality.

Every nuanced movement made greater:
their love and their passion,
their hate and their anger,
their sorrow and their joy.

As I sat in the darkened theater,
all reality was condensed and amplified.
We connected to the hive mind,
and all experienced the same emotions.

I saw my destiny
in the projector's flickering lights—
I was to live in celluloid!

II. The Odyssey's Beginning

As I left my small Idahoan town
three months shy of my eighteenth birthday,
the Greyhound went by the Main Street cinema.

I said goodbye to my temple of film,
and began my odyssey to join the gods.

III. Someone in the Crowd

With my eyes full of stars
and hope for the future,
I moved into a hostel.
My housemates were fellow worshipers.

I focused on developing my craft
by polishing the small aptitude
I had shown in high school
as one polishes a gem.

I wanted to amplify my inner fire.

As other girls were tempted by quick money
and sold their bodies on the street,
I focused on my dream.

I'd go to parties and try to meet the right people.
In this business, it's all about who you know.

At one such party
while shooting a line
from the community bowl,
I heard about a producer
who was looking for someone like me.

I chatted, flirted, and giggled
while trying to keep the innocence in my eyes.

"Take this card.
Your meeting is at the Roosevelt:
Tomorrow, room 1208, 8 pm.
At the front desk, ask for Janet.
She will take you up.
Don't be late."

As I returned home,
my feet did not touch the ground.
The time of my elevation had come.

IV. At the Roosevelt

$\mathfrak{I}$ had arrived early,
around 30 to 40 minutes,
and burned off my nervous energy
by pacing around the lobby.
I must have worn a trench in the marble.

At five 'til eight,
I approached the front desk,
clutching the key to my future,
careful not to bend it.

"How may I assist you?"

"Yes. Is Janet available?"

After my query,
the clerk gave me a knowing look,
and picked up the phone.

I watched as his fingers dialed 1... 2... 0... 8.

"I have someone to come up."

" ... "

*"She's a beautiful blonde,
nice figure, not too tall."*

"..."

"*Ok. I'll tell her.*"

With a practiced fluid movement,
he placed the handset
back in its cradle with a clack.

"*Go to the back of the lobby
where the private elevators are.
Janet is on the twelfth floor.*"

My line of sight
followed to where
his fingers directed.

As I moved away,
I felt his eyes undressing me: I didn't care.
My chance to be noticed had arrived.

V. The Audition

After riding to the floor,
the elevator door slid open.
I found Janet waiting for me.

She greeted me with a bright smile
and leaned in for a professional hug.

"Mr. Westinghouse is waiting for you.
He's heard a lot about you,
and is excited for your meet and greet."

I nodded in agreement.

"He has a causal approach,
and likes to see how well people take direction."

"Thank you for your help."

A ball of butterflies fluttered in my stomach
as if I was floating down the hallway.

With a soft knock,
Janet opened the door
and entered to announce my arrival.
I was left standing with my thoughts.

After a few moments,
Janet reemerged
and held the door.

"Go into the sitting area.
Mr. Westinghouse will join you shortly."

She slinked out the door
with it clicking closed behind her.

I stood in the center of the room
with my hands cupped in front of me
and absorbed the atmosphere.

Scented candles placed around
at strategic points in between muted lamps
exhaled a flowery perfume scent.

Muffled sounds from the bathroom
echoed through to my ears.

As he entered the room,
he closed his flapping white robe.
I caught sight of his pale naked skin
and his flaccid manhood.

He smiled at me as he sat on the sofa.
"So... You want to be in movies?"

The joy of hope bubbled through my body.

"Yes. Yes. It's my lifelong dream!
I cannot wait for the chance."

He began to explain his vision
for the new picture that he was financing
and drew me into his fantasy.

He said I was to be a slave girl,
and I needed to look the part.

After slipping out of my blouse and skirt,
I stood in my panties with an excited quiver.

"This is a seduction scene.
You are trying to win your freedom…

Here.
Move in front of me.
Get on your knees.

Now.
What would you do?
Follow your instincts…"

I closed my eyes
and pictured myself
outside my body.

When my eyes reopened,
I was a new person.

I traced my hands over his legs
feeling as his hair follicles tingled.

I moved up his flesh
and pushed the robe aside
to reveal his throbbing cock.

Starting my tongue at his knee,
I followed the pathway to his crotch.

I licked the edge of his balls and up his shaft
to where a drop of gleaming liquid
dripped from his head.

I wrapped my tongue around it
and tasted a salty shiver.

In the deep recess of my mind,
a little voice said,
"No. This is not the way..."
but I continued to focus on my role
and "act" out the scene.

With my lips attached around his cylinder,
I sucked in my cheeks
and took him down my throat.

A pleasurable moan rattled through his mouth.

"Fondle my balls."

As I followed his direction,
the little voice grew
and moved forward.

"No! Not this way!"
This caused my voice box to rattle,
"Nnnnn!"

He grabbed the sides of my head,
thrusting into the back of my throat
with his balls slapping my chin.

The voice,
no longer little,
found a way to escape.

A muffled
"nnnnNOooo!"
exited around his hard flesh,
but was hardly intelligible.

As he tried to readjust his hands,
I disengaged and pulled back a bit.

My voice,
freed from the obstruction,
gained volume.

"NO! NOT THIS WAY!"

He looked at me
with a shocked wonderment,
and pawed at my head.

With a fistful of hair,
he pushed my mouth
back towards his slightly deflated penis.

"Come on! Be a sport."

Unable to fight his strength,
I reached forward
and took his sack in my hand.

Voicing a voluminous
"NO!"
I pulled down in a twisting motion.

A sound of tearing paper crackled from my palm
along with a terrifying screech from his mouth.

His free hand balled into a fist
and connected with my eye socket.

My world went black
as I crumpled into the pile carpet.

Through my blurry swollen eye,
I could see him on the couch
with a spreading maroon stain.

I heard him mumble between sobs.

"You bitch.
You fucking bitch.
You're done!
Done!"

Feeling woozy.

I quickly gathered my shed clothing,
not turning my back on him.

He was like a wounded bear,
and I wasn't sure what he would do.

I crab-walked to the door
and, half-naked, made my way into the hall.

As I slumped into the wall, Janet rushed over.
She wore a mask of embarrassed knowledge.

She helped me dress,
ushered me down a service elevator,
and out a back exit. A cab waited for me.

VI. Curtain Call

$\mathfrak{I}$ spent the next fortnight
locked away in my room
healing from my trauma.

The physical damage faded quickly,
but the attack haunted my dreams.

I've never felt so foolish.
I've never felt so used.
I've never felt so betrayed.

All I wanted was to live on the screen.
All I wanted was to commune with the gods.
All I wanted… gone.

3…

2…

1…

"If you are just joining us,
you missed L———'s story of her
first experience with Hollywood's establishment.

Please listen as I ask her one final question.
You have had a successful career.
You have won numerous awards and accolades.

Why, after all these years,
why do you now come forward?"

"After my ordeal,
I had descended to depths
of great hopelessness and despair.

I need the world to know,
especially those trying to follow my path,
that it is possible to be successful
despite the obstacles placed before you,
and to be successful on your own terms.

Remember the light comes from inside you.
No one can extinguish it.
No one!"

VIII.

Whore of Babylon

Man has arrived at the end of an epoch,
or, as some say, the end of all things.
The time of golden copulations is upon us.

With nimble fingers,
I untie the sash of my scarlet and purple gown.
It crumples to the ground as I walk out of it.

The blazing sun sinks under the horizon
and reflects off the garnets, amethysts, and sapphires
decked into the fabric.

Refracted reds, blues, and greens
dance over my naked flesh.

My body is a toned masterpiece,
each muscle taut precision.
Caught in the westerly breeze,
my hair flows like flames.

With a cloth of crimson silk draped over white marble,
an altar has been prepared for my coming.
Towering torches billow grey smoke
at the five corners of an etched pentagram.

Around the star,
seven horned kings await my pleasure.
Each holds an implement for my use.

Their raw desire flows over my body
like waves pounding on a shore.

"I desire refreshment."

"Yes, Mistress."

The king nearest me
spits into the palm of his hand
and furiously stokes his cock
over a golden goblet.

Seeing his bulbous head
and veiny shaft in his fist
boils the blood in my body.

As his face convulses,
his elixir of life spills into the cup's well.
He passes the grail to me
with a sheepish grin on his face.

I take his offering with a slight bow
and savor its non-taste,
swallowing each droplet.

Opening my hand, I let the chalice drop.
As it rushes into the ground,
a warm pleasing tone emits.

I run my palms over the sculpture of my skin.
My breasts are full with hard nipples:
my stomach, firm and chiseled.

I push two fingers through the tangle of my bush,
open my lips and explore my crevasse.
They come away sticky and wet.

I walk over to the altar,
layover with my rear in the air,
and spread my legs slightly.

Pointing to my left,
I command,
"You. Come hither.
Sheath your sword inside me."

The second king walks behind me,
grabs my hips in his hands,
and penetrates me to my core.

I hold on to the edges of the altar
as his piston rams inside me.
The air between us cracks with each thrust.

I motion for another king
to take his place by my head.

He matches the rhythm of his partner
and shoves his rod in my mouth.

I breathe through my nose
as slobber courses down my chin.
His hardness fills my throat.

While in the throes of rapture,
I squeeze my thigh muscles
and bite down with my teeth.

My mouth fills with blood
as my womb fills with cum.
The king at my head screams and faints.

After spitting out his member as an offering,
I climb and stand on the altar,
holding my hands in the air.

Around me, the universe rotates.

As I pull my hands tighter together,
all creation forms into a dense spinning sphere.

Lightning strikes out of the ball of everything
and burns the flesh from the kings,
leaving their bleached bones behind.

My arms tremble from
containing the immense energy.
I pull the globe into my chest and hold tight.
Sweat beads on my forehead.

I squeeze both my hands together, palm to palm,
struggling to keep the universe in place.

The void of darkness surrounds me.
All known matter and life is contained in my hands.

Swallowing the bloody copper taste in my mouth,
I take an excruciating breath, and yell out,

"LET THERE BE LIGHT!"

while throwing my arms open towards the blackness.

With a rush of fire and wind,
I am ripped apart into the oblivion
of the expanding new universe.

I am dust.
I am eternal.
I am the great I AM.

Epilogue:

Metamorphosis

I. Preparing the Ritual

As I sit on a camp stool,
honing my staff,
I wait for the sun to set.

When twilight rises,
I will scribe a pattern of binding
to capture the spark of nature's magick.

After being prepared by the neophyte,
the sacred soil, a dark, rich loam,
lies flat, brimming with potential.

Tonight, we consecrate a new deity,
an angel of love and light.

As a blood orange beam
blinds my pupils with a flash of jade,
the edge of the horizon
cuts the sun from my view.
Twilight's chill surrounds me.

Beginning with the outer circle,
smooth and unbroken,
I pull my staff through the dirt.

Since a double border must be laid,
I scribe an inner circle counterclockwise.

The star of morning comes next:
each of its five points
held together by five lines
fills the empty space.

At the pole of this mini earth,
I trace the eye of Horus
as a rune of protection.

Twilight thickens into night,
torches are lit at the cardinal points
and I am ready for the Coven to arrive.

II. Ascension

Donning a carved horn mask,
vestments of midnight purple,
and a bejeweled dagger,
I take my place around the circle.

As we stand over the scared soil,
chanting, the moon reaches her apex.
The filament of the universe has come,
and the ceremony opens.

The light of the sun
reflects off the celestial orb
and pours over the pentagram.
The binding circles glow.

You walk into the pattern.

A hooded white cloak,
hand sewn from satin,
drapes your bare body
and shimmers in the light.

Your mother, a girl of sixteen,
served the temple as a sacred succubus,
glorifying the Goddess with her tactile talents.

Trained in the sensual arts,
she used her mind and body
to bring pleasure.

In fulfillment of prophecy,
she bedded the god of the sun
and conceived you at the Solstice.

During your birth,
a ball of fire consumed her,
burning down the natal chamber
but leaving you unscathed.

Living in the ashes of her death,
you grew up in the temple,
raised to take your place in the heavens.

Pushing back your hood,
and spreading your arms in an open embrace,
you turn your face towards the moon,
golden eyes burning bright.

A pair of handmaidens approach you,
remove your cloak,
and anoint your body in myrrh.

Oil flows over your forehead,
covering your muscular back,
across your buoyant breasts,
and drips down your shapely legs.
You glisten with a mythical sheen.

We stand with linked arms,
swaying about the circle
and sing a hymn of awakening.

Holding the Chalice of Stars to your lips,
you sip of the empyreal elixir.

As your eyes of fire roll to their whites,
you collapse to the ground
and form a tight ball.

The flesh of your back pulsates.

I step forward,
unsheathe my dagger
and, with two wide strokes,
slice through each shoulder blade.

A bellow of pain leaves your lips
as an igneous liquid bleeds,
running from your open wounds.

Moving to your knees,
you raise your arms towards the sky,
your hands formed into fists.

As buds of fire grow from your back,
agony flows over your face
and trembles through your body.

We change our song into one of support
and direct our energies into you.

With shaky legs,
you stand up, shivering.

The fiery buds expand
and transform into wings.

Opening to their full span,
the flaming feathers smolder
as your pale skin glows in their cool fire.

You have arrived.

Goddess of Love and Light,
Daughter of the Sun,
we kneel in adoration.

Your newfound godhood
makes me delirious,
bursting with happiness.

My heart fills with longing.

You glance at us and smile.
With a powerful push of your wings,
you lift into the air,
ascending to your new station.

I watch as you fly away,
your silhouette over the moon
casting a shadow upon us.

Our ritual now complete,
I sit in the center of the pentagram
and mediate on your transformation.

Notes

The dialogue in V. Innocence Unfound part II is taken from *Records of Salem Witchcraft, copied from the Original Documents*, vol. I. **Roxbury, Mass.: Privately Printed for W. Elliot Woodward, 1864. 140-142.** The Examination of Bridget Bishop at Salem Village 19. Apr. 1692.

About the Author

Andrew John Chiniche is a self-published author and poet with a vision to add magick to his readers' lives through the power of poetic storytelling. On his lifelong quest of higher truth, he also strives to embolden deep-rooted emotions, inspire deep thought, and invite others to ponder the mysteries of this expansive universe. In addition to authoring six poetry collections (*Love's Dawn*, *Gaze the Moon*, *The Ring of Azurmus*, *Remembrance of Beauty*, *Eternal Seconds and Song of Lilith*), he holds a Bachelor's degree in English Literature from Mississippi State University. When he isn't writing, Andrew enjoys getting lost in the unique worlds of movies and books.

www.ingramcontent.com/pod-product-compliance
Lightning Source LLC
Chambersburg PA
CBHW020653260626
47157CB00008B/3020